GUITARS

Roberta Baxter

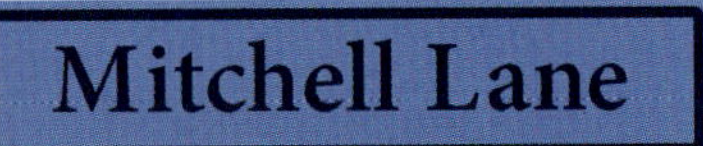

PUBLISHERS

2001 SW 31st Avenue
Hallandale, FL 33009
www.mitchelllane.com

First Edition, 2021.

Author: Roberta Baxter
Designer: Ed Morgan
Editor: Sharon F. Doorasamy

Little Mitchie is an imprint of Mitchell Lane Publishers.

Title: Musical Instruments Around the World: Guitars / by Roberta Baxter
Description: Hallandale, FL :
Mitchell Lane Publishers, [2021]

Series: Instruments Around the World
Library bound ISBN: 978-1-68020-594-7
eBook ISBN: 978-1-68020-595-4

Photo credits: pp. 4-5 Spencer Imbrock on Unsplash, p. 6 Daderot wikicommons CC0 1.0, pp. 6-7 freepik.com, pp. 8-9 Shutterstock, p. 10 Jinpisces CC-BY-SA-4.0, pp. 10-13 freepik.com, pp. 14 John Wilson/robertharding/Newscom, p. 15 Mikhail Tereshchenko/ZUMA Press/Newscom, p. 16-17 Shutterstock, p. 18 BETTMANN/REUTERS/Newscom, p. 19 (King) SMG/ZUMA Press/Newscom, p. 19 (Hendrix) KIPPA/ANP/Newscom, pp. 20-21 freepik.com

CONTENTS

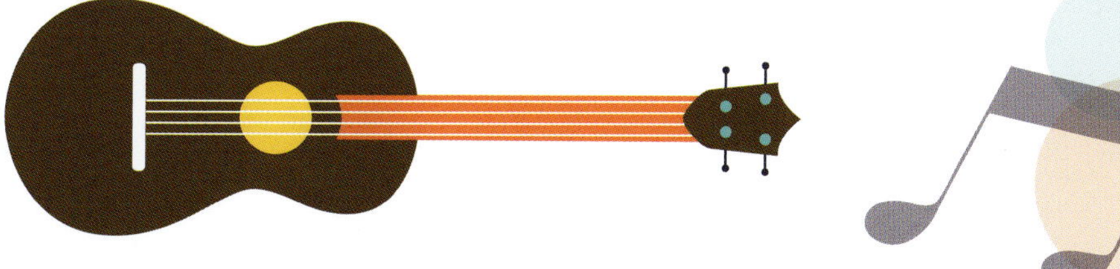

Words in **bold** can be found in the Glossary.

People everywhere love music. Sometimes the music is singing. Other times, people play **instruments**. The guitar is one of the most popular instruments in the world.

A guitar is a string instrument. Instruments similar to guitars go way back in history. In Iran, **archaeologists** found statues and carvings of guitar-like instruments that date back 3,500–4,000 years.

The *lute* is an early relative of the guitar. Egyptians, Greeks, and Romans played it. It had as many as 20 strings. The *oud* is an ancient instrument from Arabia, a vast desert peninsula in southwestern Asia. Some people think the guitar came from the lute and the oud.

Most guitars have six strings. But some have four, seven, eight, ten, or twelve strings. The strings vibrate to make sound.

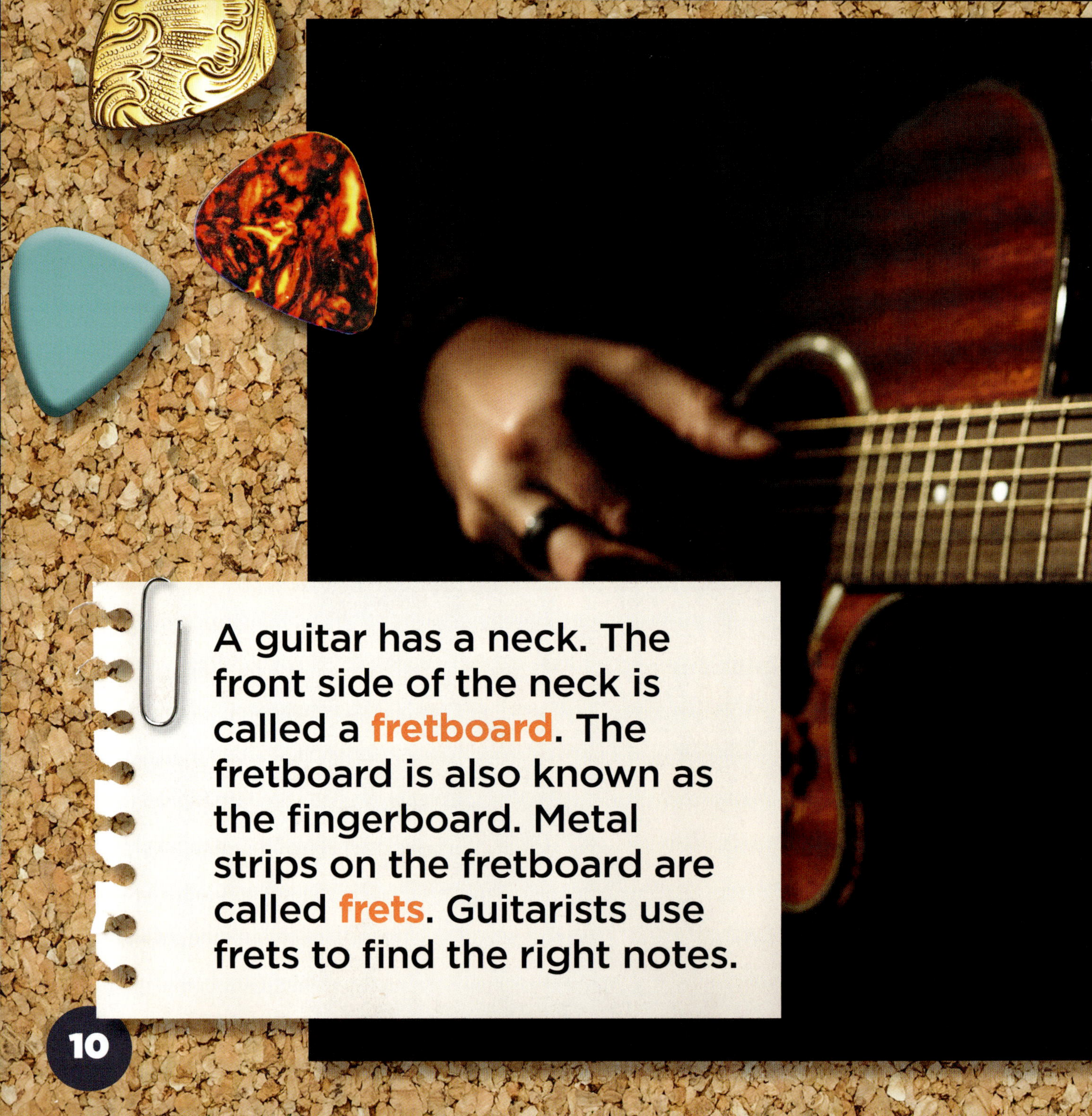

A guitar has a neck. The front side of the neck is called a **fretboard**. The fretboard is also known as the fingerboard. Metal strips on the fretboard are called **frets**. Guitarists use frets to find the right notes.

A person who plays a guitar is called a guitarist. The guitarist strums or plucks the strings with their fingers or fingernails. Sometimes guitarists use a small plastic or metal pick called a **plectrum**.

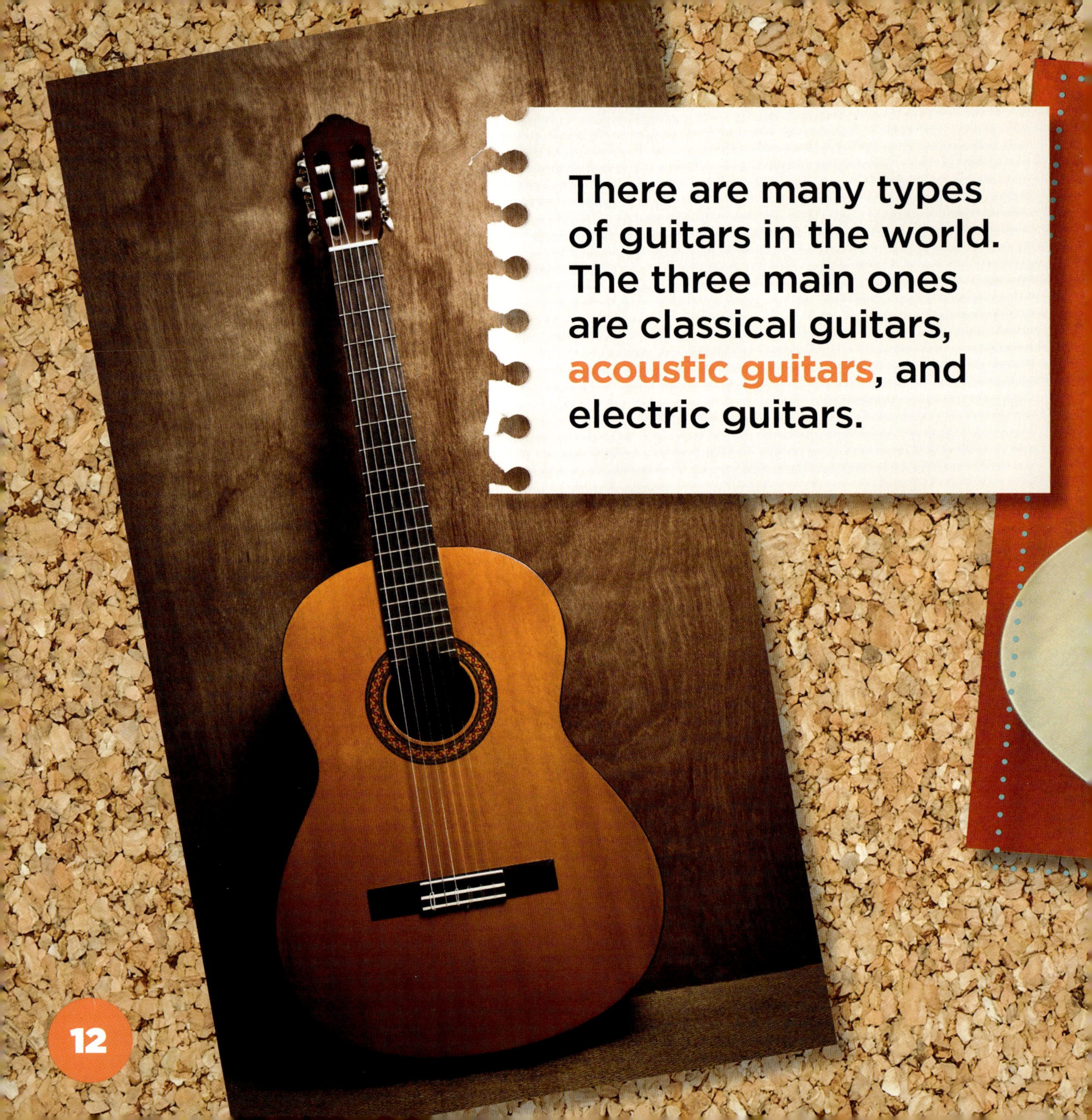

There are many types of guitars in the world. The three main ones are classical guitars, **acoustic guitars**, and electric guitars.

An instrument called the *sitar* is played in India, Pakistan, and Bangladesh. It is similar to a guitar. The *balalaika* in Russia is like a guitar. It has a triangle-shaped body and three strings.

RUSSIA
PAKISTAN
INDIA
BANGLADESH

In the 1400s, musicians in Spain began playing an instrument that looks like today's guitars. The *vihuela* had the curved body and frets. It is smaller than a guitar. The vihuela is still played in Spanish music today along with guitars.

Guitars are played in jazz, indie, rock, folk, country, heavy metal, and rhythm and blues bands. B. B. King was a famous blues guitarist. Chet Atkins was a famous country music guitarist. Guitarist Jimi Hendrix played rock music.

CHET ATKINS

B.B. KING
Merry Christmas
JIMI HENDRIX

Want to hear a guitar? Go to a concert. Listen to CDs. Even better, learn to play it yourself!

MAKE YOUR OWN GUITAR

You will need an empty cereal box, scissors, three rubber bands of different sizes, a drinking straw or pencil, a cardboard tube, and masking or duct tape.

- Decorate your box with stickers, markers, paint, or anything else you want to put on it.
- Next, cut your sound hold. To do this, trace a 3-4 inch circle in the center of one side of the cereal box. Use a jar, or any cup/glass to trace the hole. Cut it out carefully. The edges don't have to be perfect.
- Next, tape the open end of the cereal box closed. Then trace a circle on the taped end, using the cardboard tube as a guide.
- Insert the tube into the hole and secure with the tape.
- Stretch three rubber bands of different sizes over the box. Evenly space them. Tape the bands in place on the top and bottom of the box.
- Place a straw or pencil under the rubber bands below the hole (this helps with making the sound when you strum).

Try your guitar. Which of the rubber bands makes the highest note?

WHERE TO FIND FREE, USED, OR INEXPENSIVE INSTRUMENTS

- **Ask your teacher.**
- **Talk to your grandparents.** They might have some in their homes.
- **Ask the music director** at your **church**, **synagogue**, **temple**, or **mosque**.
- **Go with your parents** to **yard sales**, **flea markets**, and **secondhand shops**.
- **Ask your parents** to check **Internet websites** for discounted instruments.
- **Contact your local symphony** or a **local charity** that supports music programs.

GLOSSARY

acoustic guitar
A guitar that does not have the sound increased by an amplifier

archaeologist
Someone who studies old cultures and objects

fret
A bar across the neck of a guitar

fretboard
The neck of a guitar that has frets and against which the strings are pressed by the fingers in order to change the note that is played

indie
Music produced by a small, independent company

instrument
An object that makes music when played by a person

jazz
A type of music with strong rhythms and a mixture of instruments and singing

plectrum
A small, thin piece of plastic or metal that guitarists use to play the guitar

rhythm and blues
A type of music similar to jazz, developed by African American musicians

FURTHER READING

Amoroso, Cynthia. *Guitars*. The Child's World, 2014.

Barton, Chris. *88 Instruments*. Knopf books for Young Readers, 2016.

Evans, Gareth. *Guitar for Kids*. Intuition Publications, 2016.

Gourley, Robbin. *Talkin' Guitar: A Story of Young Doc Watson*. Clarion Books, 2015.

INDEX

ABOUT THE AUTHOR

ROBERTA BAXTER played in the school band for seven years. She doesn't play guitar, but several family members have learned the instrument after they were adults. She lives in Colorado and has written more than 45 nonfiction books for children of all ages.